Map My Home

by Jennifer Boothroyd

first step nonfiction

 captionLerner Publications Company · Minneapolis

LERNER

SOURCE™

Expand learning beyond the printed book. Download free, complementary educational resources for this book from our website, www.lerneresource.com.

The images in this book are used with the permission of: © Andersen Ross/Blend Images/Corbis, p. 4; © Todd Strand/Independent Picture Service, pp. 5, 21; © Belinda Images/SuperStock, p. 6; © iStockphoto.com/stocknroll, p. 7; © iStockphoto.com/Jenna Wagner, p. 8; © iStockphoto.com/Erin Castillo, p. 9; © iStockphoto.com/alxpin, p. 10; © iStockphoto.com/Richard Sears, p. 11; © Leremy/ Dreamstime.com, p. 12; © Laura Westlund/Independent Picture Service, pp. 13, 14, 15, 16, 17, 18, 19.

Front cover: © Laura Westlund/Independent Picture Service.

Main body text set in ITC Avant Garde Gothic Std Medium 21/25.
Typeface provided by Adobe Systems.

Lerner Publications Company
A division of Lerner Publishing Group, Inc.
241 First Avenue North
Minneapolis, MN 55401 U.S.A.

Website address: www.lernerbooks.com

Library of Congress Cataloging-in-Publication Data

Boothroyd, Jennifer, 1972–
    Map my home / by Jennifer Boothroyd.
        p.   cm. — (First step nonfiction—map it out)
    Includes index.
    ISBN 978–1–4677–1110–4 (lib. bdg. : alk. paper)
    ISBN 978–1–4677–1739–7 (eBook)
    1. Cartography—Juvenile literature. 2. Maps—Juvenile literature. I. Title.
GA105.6.B66 2014
526—dc23   2012042554

Manufactured in the United States of America
1 – PP – 7/15/13

Table of Contents

We learned about fire safety in school.

Our teacher drew a safety
plan for our classroom.

I will draw a **map** of my home. It will show the main ways out.

My map will show the rooms in our home.

It will show the outside doors.

It will show my family's meeting spot. That's where we will meet in case of fire. 9

Our meeting spot is **south** of our front door.

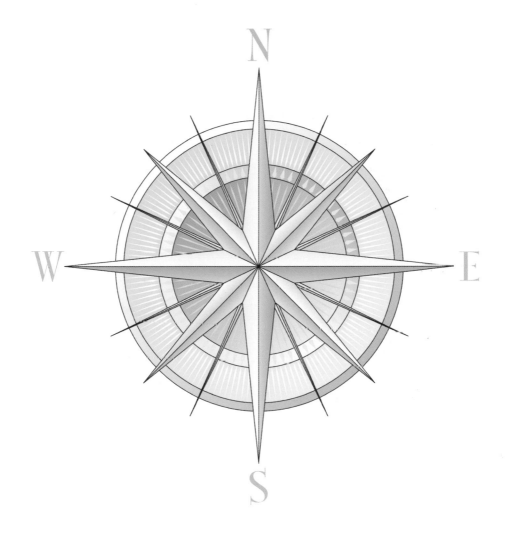

My map will have a
compass rose to show
which way is south. 11

BUS STATION

POLICE STATION

TAXI STAND

FIRE STATION

LIGHT RAIL STATION

HOSPITAL

TRAIN STATION

LIBRARY

AIRPORT

POST OFFICE

It will also have a **key**. A key helps people read a map.

I drew the **outline** of my home.

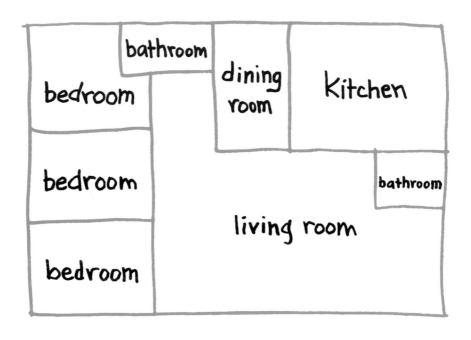

I drew in the rooms.
I wrote a **label** in each.

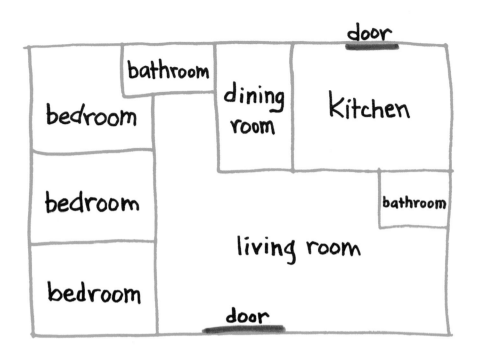

I drew the main doors.
I made them bright orange.

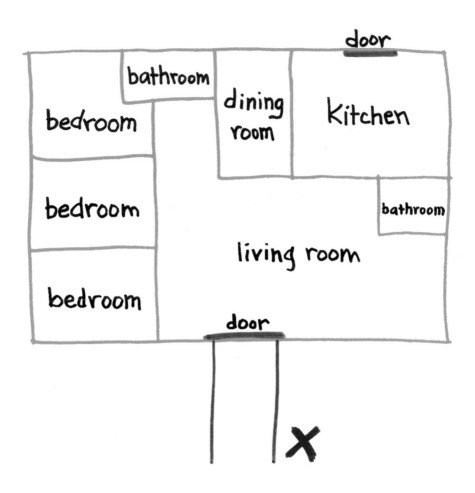

I marked the meeting spot.
I drew a big red *X*.

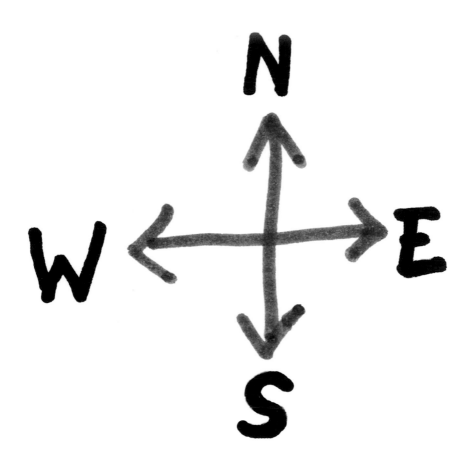

I put the compass rose in one corner.

I added the key in the
other corner.

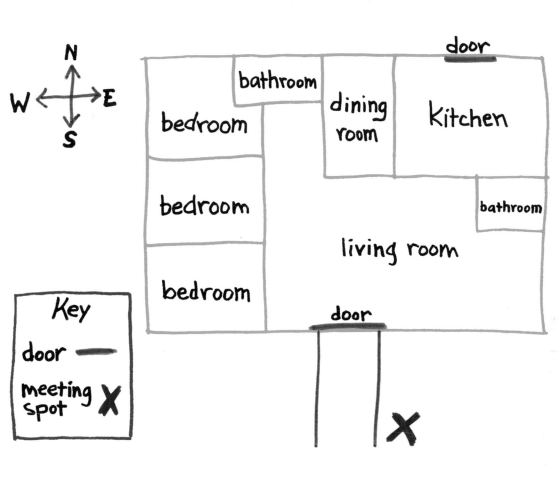

The map is done. Now it is time for our family fire drill.

How to Make a Map of Your Home

1. Decide what you will put on your map. Your map should show your home's rooms. You may also want to show doors. You could show a meeting spot if you are making a fire map.
2. Draw the outline of your home.
3. Draw in the rooms and anything else you are including. Label every room.
4. Draw in a compass rose if you want one. Draw in a key if you want one.

Fun Facts

- There are many types of homes. People live in apartments, houses, and mobile homes.

- Some apartments have only two rooms. One is a bathroom. The other is used as the kitchen, bedroom, and living room.

- A mansion is a large house. Some mansions have more than 30 rooms.

Glossary

compass rose – a drawing showing the directions on a map

key – the part of a map that explains the symbols

label – a word put on something to describe it

map – a drawing that shows where places are

outline – the shape of a place made by the outer edge

south – one of four main directions on a compass

Index